Dr. Meli

Ralph K. Rothacker

& Nathan Levy

School Leaders' Guide to Trauma Sensitive Schools

Creating Trauma Sensitive Schools from Practice to Policy

Nathan Levy Books, LLC
18 Moorland Boulevard
Monroe Township NJ 08831
www.storieswithholes.com
nlevy103@comcast.net

ISBN - 978-0-9997908-6-1

Printed in the United States of America

Cover artwork by Dallin Orr
www.dallinorr.com

Dr. Sadin dedicates this book to her husband, Andrew, who taught her that in leadership, sometimes we walk alongside, sometimes, we follow, and always, we lead with our hearts.

Mr. Rothacker dedicates this book to all the girls at St. Anne's who have taught him first-hand about understanding the traumatic effects of ACE's on life and learning. They are some of the strongest people he has ever met, and they need to be heard, supported, and deserve champions like us to right the wrongs they have so courageously endured. Ralph K. Rothacker

Nathan Levy dedicates this book to all those administrative interns, assistant principals, unit leaders and mentees who went on to exceed the high expectations he had for them under his tutelage, and training:

Dr. Cheryl Moretz - Summit Elementary School, NJ Principal and author
Scott Feder - South Brunswick, NJ Superintendent
Marci Levy-Maguire - Former principal, dynamic daughter, wonderful mother of Sadie
Joanne Levy - Art Director, dynamic daughter, wonderful mother of Nova
Kokona Chrisos – Principal, Indiana
Melissa Sadin - Former principal, current author and consultant
Gary Abbamont - Assistant Superintendent, PA
Steve Cochran – Princeton, NJ Superintendent
Dr. Linda Madison - Bound Brook, NJ Superintendent (retired)
Antoine Green - Former Teaneck, NJ Principal
Dr. Andrew Rose - Former Norwood, NJ Superintendent

Larry Mendelowitz - Former Assistant Superintendent, current college professor

Nicolle Pormilli - Assistant Superintendent Jackson NJ

Dr. James Singagliese – Bridgewater, NJ Principal

JoAnne Kerekes - Former Assistant Superintendent, South Brunswick, NJ

Glenn Famous - Former South Brunswick, NJ Principal

Dr. Donna Johnson - Author, current Assistant Director Harlem's Children Zone

Dr. Thomas Howard - College of New Jersey Program Director

Mark Kmiec -Assistant Principal South, Brunswick NJ

Cathy Yorke - Assistant Principal Marlboro, NJ

Michele Waldron - Assistant Principal Cranbury NJ,

Celeste Gagliardi - Director of Programs

Paul Sears - Summit High School NJ Principal, retired, author

Adam Laningham – Author, Director of Gifted, Deer Valley, AZ

Denise Touhey - Former Principal South Brunswick, NJ

Becky Gensel - Superintendent, Branchburg, NJ

Rick Chromey -Former Assistant Superintendent

Lynette Dortrait - Jersey City Assistant Principal

Lynne Fox - Lead Consultant for Leader and Me

Lem Perez – Principal, Jersey City, NJ

Scott Hobson – Assistant Principal, Millstone, NJ

Gary Yepez – Unit Leader, South Brunswick, NJ

Kristen Higgins – Principal, Three Bridges, NJ

Last, but most importantly, the person who continues to train me - my wife, Dominique Zuani-Levy

Forward by Dr. Timothy Purnell

Former National Association of School Superintendents (NASS) National Superintendent of the Year, Professor of Mental Health and Ethics, and the Chief Executive Officer of the American Montessori Society.

I had the honor and privilege of serving alongside Dr. Melissa Sadin as she served on the school board during my time as superintendent of Somerville Public Schools, New Jersey. As a board, one of our strategic priorities focused on cultural competency and addressing a growing dropout rate within the district. Dr. Sadin provided the board, leadership team, community, and me with a better understanding of the importance of creating a trauma-informed systemic approach to learning within schools. Upon hearing the positive outcomes of this approach, our district immediately began work to achieve this goal.

As a direct result of her efforts and the boards' desire to meet the needs of our children, the district became one of the first trauma-informed school districts in the state of New Jersey. All staff (including substitute teachers, bus drivers, and consultants) were trained in a trauma-informed approach to children. Additionally, the district launched a new high school designed to mitigate the impact of adverse childhood experiences (ACEs). Thanks to the efforts of our incredibly talented staff, the support of the board, and the hard work of Dr. Sadin, the new high school and trauma-informed approach led to tremendous recognition at the state and national level, which resulted in requests for professional development and speaking engagements.

In this book, the authors lay out the psychological and neurobiological impact that trauma has on child development and provide the "WHY" and "HOW" to create a trauma-informed environment in schools (from policy to practice). I can personally attest that Dr. Sadin was directly responsible for analyzing each of the Somerville school district policies and procedures to ensure an intentional commitment to a trauma-informed approach. The case studies in this book provide readers with real life scenarios and specific illustrations of the situations that leaders will face during the implementation of this approach.

The authors also place an emphasis on the importance of self-care and the care of the staff working in trauma-informed schools. According to the authors, the school-wide practices identified in this book have demonstrated increased staff attendance and created an overall positive working environment for employees. Providing a healthy work environment and genuine care of staff have been critical to my personal success as a leader.

Introduction

From Dr. Sadin

One in four children in every classroom, everyday has been exposed to some form of childhood trauma. It is time for a REVOLUTION! Webster defines a revolution as the "forcible" overthrow of a system. Our revolution is more of a peaceful movement. Gandhi once said that, "A non-violent revolution is a program of relationships ending in a peaceful transfer of power." It should be peaceful and relationship building, rather than violent and relationship ending. A peaceful revolution is no less urgent than a violent one.

As most of our readers know, "We cannot keep doing what we have always done, or we will keep getting what we have always gotten." School shootings are on the rise. Our children are killing people! Every school shooter since Eric Harris and Dylan Klebold at Columbine High School was a child of trauma. The path to a reduction in school shootings is not with more guns. This is not about guns or our Constitutional right to bear arms. It is about children. It is about trauma. The path to a reduction in school shootings and better schools is through trauma-informed schools. A peaceful revolution.

Imagine that schools are ponds. In the ponds are ducks. Ducks of many shapes and sizes. Ducks with autism. Ducks with dyslexia. Gifted ducks. We have become very good in this country at educating ducks. The problem is that in our ponds, among the ducks, sit lions. Lions cannot be cared for the same way as you would care for a duck. They need different food and a different environment. If you leave a lion to be raised in a duck pond, she or he will do one of three things: Freeze – stop trying to eat the duck food and eventually die; Flee – leave the pond in search of tall grass and meat; or Fight – eat the other ducks. What they will never do is become ducks.

If you have been in education for five or more years, then all of your pre-service teaching instruction was through the lens of social learning theory (SLT). Social learning theory was developed in the 1970s. It is based on the premise that as humans we are social animals, and we learn by observing others. Much of Bandura's work on self-efficacy is the foundation of many of our current Social Emotional Learning programs (SEL). SEL presumes that all children have typical and appropriate prefrontal cortex development. Recent breakthroughs in medical technology have allowed researchers to see that children who experience trauma have brains that are not the same as children who do not experience trauma. (More about this in chapter 3). Most schools across the country can be explained by the tiers in that school. The three tiers came from the Response to Intervention framework and are also used by Positive Behavior Support (PBS) programs. Tier I encompasses all programs that are good for all. It is basically general education. All programs in Tier I are available to all. Like Oxygen. It is there for all. No one has to ask for it. The curriculum is Tier I. Tier II is good for some. It is the intervention tier. Generally, the programs in Tier II require some sort of performance score to access. For example, some general education reading intervention programs where students must score at or below a certain cut off are eligible for the program. Tier III is good for a few. Entrance into these programs requires rigorous assessment, like special education.

Our schools are set up, from the curriculum and social emotional learning in Tier 1 to special education in Tier 3, to address the needs of children with the assumption that they all have the same neurological capacity for learning. The assumption is that they are all ducks. We now know that in our ponds among the ducks are lions. They cannot thrive in the same environment. They will never be ducks. If we create schools that are also good for lions, the ducks will perform even better than they do now. Trauma-informed schools are good for ALL. Trauma-informed schools use the good work of previous educational leaders and innovators and build upon it with an understanding of the recent breakthroughs in the neurobiology of trauma.

Our current system of education (the duck pond approach) is not working for all children. Our academic achievement is good, but not great. We are under serving our gifted children (read the book co-authored by Adam Laningham, Dr. Melissa Sadin and Nathan Levy called *Gifted Children & How Trauma Impacts Them*). We are under serving our *lions*. Take a look at your school data. Who is in the achievement gap? Are they children of color? Immigrants? Children living in poverty? Children of trauma ARE many of the children in the achievement gap. We have been spending countless hours and dollars researching, developing, and implementing fantastic remedial curricula. I have been in public school education for over thirty years. I learned about the achievement gap in my first year of teaching. I learned to write SMART goals. Every year there was a goal aimed at closing the achievement gap. Thirty years later as a school leader, I am still looking at the achievement gap. We cannot keep doing what we have always done, or we will keep getting what we have always gotten.

A Note to my Fellow School Board Members

This book is as much for you as it is for the employed leaders of your school district. As you read, consider your fellow board members as your colleagues. Learn to recognize and identify the role of your superintendent, executive director, principals, and members of the central office administration. They will need your support in this revolution. They will need direction in the form of district goals. They will need resources in the form of time and money. But most importantly, they will need you to make sure they are taking care of themselves so they can take care of the students. Throughout the book, we will make specific reference to you and your connection to certain topics of discussion. In addition, the information in the data section and the policy section is for you. Thank you for volunteering to serve. Thank you for caring for the children in your city or town!

The format of this book follows the 4 R's of a trauma-informed organization (school) as defined by the Substance Abuse and Mental Health Service Administration (SAMHSA 2017). A trauma-informed school is one where everyone in the community REALIZES the prevalence of trauma, RECOGNIZES the impact of trauma on neurobiological Development, RESPONDS in a trauma-informed way, and RESISTS RETRAUMATIZATION. In the pages that follow, we will explain each stage and provide examples for creating a trauma-informed school.

It is time for a peaceful revolution! Congratulations! You have joined us in our revolution by reading this book!

From Mr. Rothacker

A Note to School Leaders

Congratulations! The fact that you are reading this demonstrates that you have taken one of the most critical steps in transforming your organization into a trauma sensitive environment. Children need more people like you to champion this movement towards establishing classrooms and schools which have students feeling safe and emotionally connected as prerequisites to learning.

There is no question that Adverse Childhood Experiences (ACEs) can have a dramatic negative impact on learning and long-term health. We know that in our classrooms almost half of our students have experienced at least one ACE, and many have significantly more. The data on ACEs shows that childhood trauma is a national epidemic. The research is clear that exposure to Adverse Childhood

Experiences is a dose-response relationship. The more ACEs you have, the more it impacts your adult health outcomes. (More on ACEs in Chapter 2). As educational leaders, we cannot ignore the dramatic impact ACEs have on the social and emotional well-being of our students. We must make this the first order of business. Simply put, students do not have the capacity to learn when their minds are preoccupied with safety and survival.

Some suggest that trauma is reaching crisis status in our nation and should be addressed as a public health crisis. I would agree. The good news is that we know that the human brain is malleable and can be rewired under the right conditions, and this is where you come in. Our kids need you more than ever right now to create those conditions in your school where students feel safe, valued and in control of their emotions. Only then will meaning-ful learning take place.

Be the *First* and *Last* in Line

As school leaders, we are at the forefront of any and all initiatives that our schools embark upon. We must be the catalyst for change by clearing the path and setting the stage for excellence to happen. Conversely, we must also be prepared to be the trailer and identify any critical components of the initiative that are not being addressed.

The same holds true when you are creating a genuine trauma based school program. School leaders need to be the first in line to model trauma sensitive interactions; not only in their office but in the halls, classrooms, cafeteria, playground, and staff meetings. I know that school leaders are often tethered to their desk inundated with paperwork that needs to get done. However, I can attest that MBWA (Management By Walking Around) is a crucial step in transforming your school.

Although educators are reluctant to admit it, there are some students that are almost impossible to like. These students can be rude, obnoxious, noncompliant, self-centered and repel any type of adult interactions. As a leader, these are the very students YOU want/need to reach out to; the ones that no one else gravitates towards. If you can find a way to take on the most challenging student(s), and get them to make a change for the better, imagine the impact it would have on your staff! Think about it. What do you have to lose? If you are successful, you have set an example for your staff that meaningful relationships can be developed with the most challenging students. However, if your connection with the student is taking longer than anticipated, people will still witness and appreciate your efforts. Notice I did not say, "If your connection with the student is failed...." Failure only happens when you stop trying. Remain steadfast in your belief that it will happen.

Trauma informed leadership starts and ends with you.

From Nathan Levy

This book is written by three practitioners who have had high levels of success as participants in central office roles, as school principals, as school board members, and as presidents of state organizations. Together, they have written more than sixty books used by educators at all levels. The focus of our work and our guidance is to assure that all children get the opportunity to reach their maximum potential. All ducks and lions deserve to have great school experiences. Children who always do "the right thing" deserve recognition and awards. All children, regardless of their life experiences, abilities, and/or family circumstances, deserve to get the best we can offer. We care about ALL children and have written books to help educators and care givers support all different types of students succeed. We do not want these points to be lost in our focus in this book on the large number of varied types of children we work with every day.

Change Leadership

In the past 25 years, two models of leadership have dominated the research; instructional leadership and transformational leadership. Instructional leadership is characterized by school leaders who prioritize coordinating, controlling, supervising, and developing curriculum. This form of leadership gained notoriety when studies showed that strong focus on curriculum and instruction was bringing about positive academic gains in urban settings. Transformational leadership is characterized by school leaders who prioritize building their organization's capacity for change. Transformational leadership is change leadership.

Social justice is a construct built on respect, care, recognition, and empathy. It can be defined as the exercise of altering organizational climate by actively engaging in reclaiming and advancing inherent human rights of equity, equality, and fairness in social, economic, educational, and personal dimensions. School leaders with a high degree of social justice have been shown to make issues of race, class, gender, disability, sexual orientation, and other marginalizing conditions central to their advocacy, practice and vision.

Creating trauma-informed schools requires leaders who possess a solid foundation in curriculum and instruction, the ability to build capacity for change, and a high level of social justice. Our schools must have a solid, culturally competent curriculum for our teachers to implement. Our teachers need to apply the curriculum through the use of evidence based and highly effective instructional strategies. Leaders in trauma-informed schools must also support and encourage change in the form of a paradigm shift. A shift toward cultural competence. A shift from crime and punishment to behavior response and repair. A shift from "What is wrong with you?" to "What has happened to you?" Research shows that leaders who possess a high level of social justice are more successful at shifting paradigms.

Dr. Sadin's doctoral research focused on the perspectives of teachers who were creating trauma-informed classrooms. The participants in the study shared a few common needs. They mentioned a need for their school counselors to understand the psychological and neurobiological impact of trauma on children. They mentioned the need for more training regarding creating trauma-informed education for themselves and their colleagues. However, the number one thing that all the participants voiced as their greatest need was a principal who understood and supported trauma-informed schools. Studies currently tracking the programs and outcomes of schools becoming trauma-informed are also noting that, ultimately, the single, most important ingredient for creating trauma-informed schools is a change leader. Schools with a change leader with a high level of social justice are the schools that are meeting with the most success. In schools where a teacher, a few teachers, or a school counselor, are responsible for the transformation, the movement cannot be sustained. Teachers are burning out or leaving their district to find a place where they can be supported in their trauma-informed efforts.

Trauma-informed school leaders create a community where everyone accepts the students' past, supports their present, and encourages their futures. You are school leaders. You can do this. The fate of our revolution depends on you!

Nathan Levy adds this note of advice "On Being a Changemaker" that he has periodically shared in his workshops. The originator of the statement is Karen Pryor.

On Being a Changemaker

A biologist's look at the process of making change

An animal trainer named *Karen Pryor* wrote this essay. It has broad applicability beyond her field of work ...such as the education and well-being of children.

What people do when you start to institute change (in chronological order):

1. Ignore you
2. Pretend to agree, but actually do nothing
3. Resist, delay, obstruct
4. Openly attack you (the dangerous phase, but also a sign that change is starting)
5. Absorb
6. Utilize
7. Take credit
8. Proselytize

What people say in the process of accepting change:

- "That might work for your population but not for mine." (absorbing)
- "I can use it, but not for anything important." (absorbing and utilizing)
- "Some of my people can use it if they feel they need to." (utilizing)

- "Oh yes, we've been doing that for years, it's quite good." (utilizing and taking credit)
- "We've come up with a really incredible program: you should try it." (taking credit and proselytizing)

How the changemaker can react effectively

- When they ignore you, find allies and persist.
- Don't be misled by lip service. Find allies and persist.
- Meet resistance with persistence. Move around the resistance; try other avenues.
- The stage of open attack is a touch time. People can get fired, for example. Keep your head down, but persist. Don't take the attack personally, even if it is a personal attack. Attack is information; it tells you something:
    a. You're getting somewhere; change IS happening, causing extinction induced aggression
    b. Your attacker is frightened. Empathize.
    c. Your attacker still believes in the efficacy of aversives.
- Absorbing and utilizing: this stage can last a year or more. Maintain generous schedules of reinforcement.
- They're taking credit for your idea? By all means, let them: your goal is the change. Credit is a low-cost reinforce and people who want it don't satiate. Give it away in buckets.
- Are they pitching the change to others? Good. If you want to change something else, you now have new allies.

1

The First R - Realize the Prevalence of Trauma

A study conducted in the early 1990's found that 30% of the female and 40% of the male participants reported multiple forms of maltreatment in childhood. Ten years ago, a study reported that more than one in four school aged children reported at least one form of childhood maltreatment. Three years later, that number was increased to almost half of school aged children reporting at least one form of maltreatment.

The study that blew the lid off this widespread problem was originally conducted more than twenty years ago by Dr. Robert Anda, Dr. Vincent Felitti, and their team. The survey they administered to 17,000 college students was called the Adverse Childhood Experiences study (ACEs). They asked each participant ten questions about their childhood. Each time a participant replied yes to a question, they counted an ACE. Sixty-four percent of the participants replied yes to at least one adverse childhood experience. (The original survey and updated versions of

the study are available as free downloads at
www.acestoohigh.com.) The results of this study
demonstrated the overwhelming prevalence of childhood
trauma. Further study showed that there are clear
negative adult health outcomes that can be predicted
based on the number of adverse childhood experiences
(ACEs) reported by the individual. People who report
three or more ACEs report an increase in heart disease,
cancer, mental illness, and substance abuse (Anda et al.,
2010). The following picture shows the predictable
health outcomes reported by adults with three or more
ACEs.

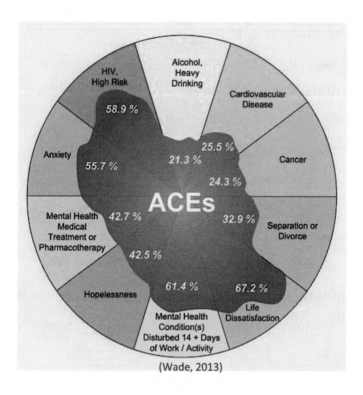

(Wade, 2013)

Continuing studies by Dr. Anda and Dr. Felitti and a host of other researchers show that there is great hope for success in this work. Follow-up studies show that when people become aware of their ACE score and take steps to address their health concerns, they may greatly improve their outcomes. In other words, what is predictable is often preventable.

After all of this research, it is safe to say that there are children in every school in our country who have been exposed to adverse childhood experiences. This is not just an urban problem. This is not just a rural poor problem. Children are experiencing maltreatment in every community in our country. Children grow up and become teachers and school leaders. It is possible that half of your adult school community were children who experienced maltreatment. (More on caring for your adult lions in chapter 5.) This is a national epidemic. The time for change is now.

The Use of ACEs in Schools

We do not recommend that the ACEs survey be given to any child under the age of twelve. We are also not suggesting that you greet every student at the door on the first day of school and hand them a survey. It is important to understand that as educators, we do not need to know exactly how many ACEs a child has to be able to provide an appropriate learning experience. One teacher can believe that a student has six ACEs. Another may believe the student has ten. It does not matter. What does matter is knowing that the child has likely had exposure to adverse experiences. Remember, creating Trauma-Informed schools is good for **all** children. We do recommend, however, that over the course of time, you explain ACEs and adult health outcomes to every adult in your community. Care givers, bus drivers, paraprofessionals, custodians, administrative assistants, and school board members all benefit from knowing their ACE score. Presenting a workshop or parent night on ACEs is a great way to kick off your trauma-informed movement. Present it as a national health crisis and public service announcement. It lands much better than standing up at open house and announcing that your school or district is becoming trauma informed. Keep in mind, one size fits one. We have seen school leaders do just that - Stand up and tell everyone that trauma-informed practices and procedures are their priority. The authors have all known and worked in districts and communities where a statement about *trauma*-informed education begged the question, "Wait. We have trauma in our town?" You know your community and what will work best for them.

We also recommend that your school counselors, school psychologists, and social workers get trained and are familiar with ACEs and the survey. There is a survey, for example, for high school girls where the language and the content are suitable for young adult women. We have worked with schools where the counselor or psychologist, working with an individual middle or high school student, may administer the survey as a way to help them understand themselves and learn to take care of their needs based on their trauma exposure. School social workers can collect ACEs information through the social history conducted as a part of the evaluation for special education. We consulted in a school that spent a year providing one-hour ACEs workshops to care givers, community members, and staff. In addition, they secured and expanded their relationships with community child welfare and municipal service providers. The next year, they put the ACEs survey in the kindergarten orientation packets with the word "optional" written in large letters at the top. The objective was to collect any data they could on their incoming students. Many surveys were returned. Care givers want someone to help their children even if they might be part of the problem. It is also important to note that we, as educators, are in the business of helping to heal families. That is not, however, our main job. We need support and collaboration from our community service providers. As you will learn in the next chapter, there is a correlation between the number

of ACEs our students have, and their capacity for learning.
That is our business.

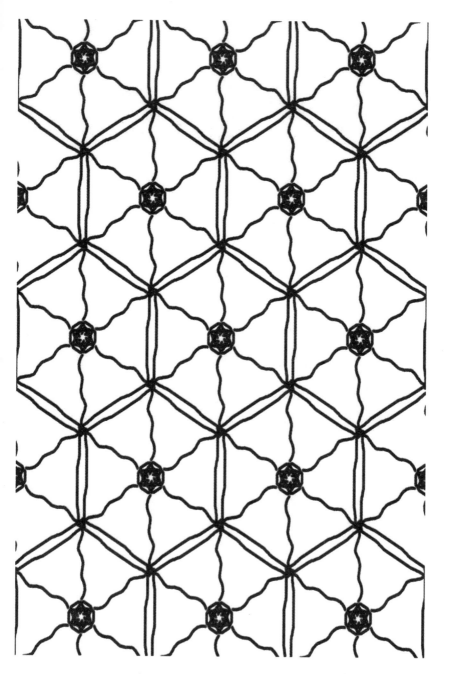

Coloring pages designed by Ally T. Cohen

2

The Second R - RECOGNIZE the Impact of Trauma

Children who have prolonged exposure to trauma in childhood, including but not limited to family violence, physical, emotional or sexual abuse, separation from a primary caregiver, and poverty are considered to have *developmental* trauma. This type of trauma exposure may impair neurobiological development. Prolonged exposure to early childhood trauma causes atypical development of the amygdala, hippocampus, and prefrontal cortex. The amygdala and hippocampus are important parts of our limbic system that are necessary for, among other things, emotional control, language development, memory, reasoning, and cognition.

In typical development, all children are amygdala driven at birth. The amygdala is also known as our survival brain. It is responsible for our survival behaviors. Human infants are completely unable to survive alone. If you put an infant in a field alone, eventually, he or she will not survive without assistance. Babies cannot keep themselves warm. They cannot feed themselves. They cannot drink by themselves. They need another human to provide their basic needs. The amygdala is what causes babies to cry. They cry when they are hot. They cry when they are cold. They cry when they are hungry. They cry when they are thirsty. They cry when they are afraid. They cry when they are lonely. They cry as a way to bring another human to help them. If you have ever raised a baby or been close to someone who has, then you know that it is a pretty good system. When a baby cries, we respond. We pick him up. We ask him, "What is wrong?" We hold him, bounce him, check his diaper, check the time to decide if he is hungry or thirsty. While we are going through our checklist of what might be wrong, very often we are telling him that he will be alright. We tell him, "It is okay." When we do this over and over thousands of times over two to three years, the amygdala responds less, and the hippocampus gets busy. The hippocampus is the center for things such as emotional self-regulation, language development, and memory. The activity in the hippocampus helps us realize that every discomfort is not life threatening. We can be hungry. It is okay. We will get food soon. We are cold. It is okay. We can get a coat or move to a warmer place. We begin to do for ourselves what our care givers did for us when we were infants. Over the next ten to fifteen years, when we continue to have a safe place where our basic needs are met, our prefrontal cortex comes online. With the prefrontal cortex comes the ability to manage delayed gratification, choice, empathy, reasoning, and judgement.

Children with trauma have atypical limbic system development. Often, they do not get their basic needs met as infants, babies, and toddlers. Their amygdala remains in charge. They are constantly on alert for perceived threats to their safety. With recent medical advances and the development of the functional magnetic resonance imaging (fMRI) machine, neurobiologists, scientists, and medical doctors have been able to study the response centers in the brains of living human subjects in real time without endangering the safety of the subject. Research shows that children with trauma often have larger amygdala and smaller hippocampus volume than children without trauma. It is important to understand that this means that children in a fifth grade class may have the prefrontal cortex activity of a four year old. High school students who have experienced trauma may have the judgement of a fifth grader. Brains cannot skip stages of development. A child cannot do more than his/her brain development allows. Children who are amygdala driven cannot choose their behavior. Sixteen-year-old young adults with developmental trauma may not choose a healthy peer group. They may not make age appropriate decisions while operating a vehicle. They may not be able to wait their turn in class the way a child without trauma can.

We can understand the neurobiology of trauma by studying the limbic system. We can understand the psychology of trauma by learning about attachment. Many children with trauma histories also have attachment disruption or fragile attachment as a result of absent or inconsistent care. Attachment occurs while we are picking our babies up, holding them, telling them they will be okay, and looking at them. Attachment develops when we stare forever, fascinated by our babies' faces. Attachment happens when we feed our children dinner every night. Children with trauma may have intermittent experience with parental gazing. They may have begun forming healthy attachment that is interrupted by a care giver who is no longer physically or emotionally available. This results in delayed development of the internal working model (IWM). Internal working models are necessary for the development of self. Children with fragile attachment may not have a fully developed sense of self. This interferes with their ability to develop self-regulation, self-determination, and self-efficacy. *Self, self, self.* You need a self to develop any of these capacities. Children without an internal working model have a skewed or absent sense of self.

Establishing relationships is necessary for survival. We, as humans, are social animals. We do not survive well alone. Children with fragile attachment may have difficulty establishing relationships because a functioning internal working model is necessary for the development of trust - Trust with a capital T. Children without trauma exposure, who are firmly attached, go to school trusting that someone there will help them if they have a problem.

Consider this example from Dr. Sadin in her role as Mom: I have had the joy and the challenge of raising both an adopted son and a biological son. My husband and I found our eldest son, Theo, in a Bulgarian orphanage when he was three years old. When he was five, I gave birth to our second son, Noah. In addition to the extreme satisfaction I found in motherhood, I found I had a clinic in attachment playing out in my home. Noah's attachment process was seamless and natural. He knew my voice the day he arrived. I remember when he began to track me in the room with his eyes. In addition to me, my husband, mother- in-law, and sisters were all happy to rush to Noah the minute he made a sound. Caregivers who are creating secure attachment respond to their babies when they cry. We may not always guess what is troubling our infants, but we always <u>try</u>. It is in the consistent trying, cooing, soothing, and laughter that secure attachment develops. Theo's (my older son) attachment process was not as seamless. His attachment struggles seemed to come from two wildly different places. One was, "Can I TRUST you?" His amygdala driven brain was ever on alert for threats to his survival. Remember, he was left in an orphanage by his birth mother. He had no reason to believe and no way to understand that his placement in our home was permanent. His other attachment approach was, "I am unworthy of love." This caused him to feel deep, deep shame when he did something wrong. When we took Noah to a park or playground, he would look to see where we were. If he lost sight of us, he would cry or come looking. When we took Theo to a park or playground, for years, it was our job to watch him. He rarely looked for us. I remember the day, when he was about eight years old, that he looked for me for the very first time. We were at the beach. Theo was very busy driving his little red truck into the hole we dug in the sand. Noah wandered too close to the water, so I jumped up to stand near him. I saw Theo look up to my beach chair, and not finding me sitting there, stood up to search for me. I called to him, and he came over and hugged me. That memory still makes me tear up. He was trying SO hard. It was working. He knew I was his mother. My husband and I spent many years firming up our attachment to Theo. We cannot undo the effects of neglect, abuse, and fragile attachment in the early years of a child's life. But we can work with what we have and make small gains every day.

Attachment in School

Noah was nervous his first day of preschool. But he marched into his new classroom with the knowledge born of secure attachment. He TRUSTED that if he needed help, his teacher would be there to assist. He was wearing what Dr. Sadin calls his "red cape of attachment." Conversely, Theo had to be pulled off her leg by his caring (and strong) teacher on his first day of preschool. He did not trust that his needs would be met. He did not trust that he would ever see his mother again.

Teachers can be attachment figures. When they understand and learn to identify fragile attachment, their consistent acceptance and empathy can teach children to attach in healthy ways. (More on this in Chapter 3).

A Note about Vocabulary

Think of ACEs and developmental trauma as synonyms. A child with six ACEs does have developmental trauma. A child with developmental trauma has more than six ACEs. As educators, we work to avoid diagnosing children. A child may appear to have difficulty with focus, and we try not to say that the child has ADHD. The good news in this work is that saying a child has ACEs or saying a child has developmental trauma is not offering a diagnosis. We believe that one day soon, Developmental Trauma Disorder will be in the official book of all mental illnesses, the Diagnostic and Statistical Manual (DSM). The term developmental trauma is a description that affords us a set of learning characteristics. It is not a diagnosis.

3

The Third R - RESPOND in a Trauma-Informed Way

When we train teachers about creating trauma sensitive schools, we use the framework - create safety, connection, regulation, and learning (SAMHSA, 2017).

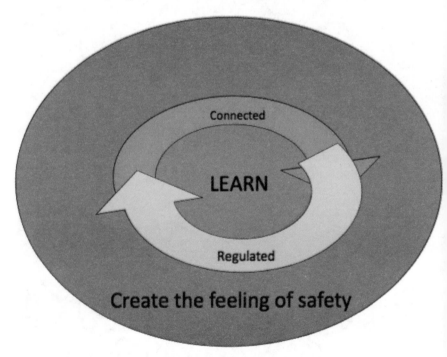

The Attachment & Trauma Network, 2017

Safety

Safety in the Classroom

Children who have experienced adverse experiences and/or have fragile attachment do not feel safe on a molecular level. That is to say that they do not naturally possess what we call "three-dimensional safety." One dimensional safety is derived from knowing your environment. The doors of the school are locked. Visitors must enter and be greeted by someone at the main entrance. Ducks and lions can feel one dimensional safety by looking around and knowing the rules. Three-dimensional safety is much deeper. Am I safe from judgement? Do people like me? Am I good enough? Do people accept me? Will anyone help me? Children who have their needs met, emotionally and physically, develop three-dimensional safety as they grow. Their arena of safety grows with them. Little babies learn to tolerate longer times without their mothers in the room with them. Elementary school children might be having their first sleepover at a friend's house. Middle school children show an interest in spending more time with their friends than with their care givers. They are safe. They know they are loved which helps them believe they are worthy. They are safe to take the risks associated with learning. They can sound out a word they have never seen. They can learn from their mistakes. They are curious about the world around them. They know where to go if they need help. Children who do not have their needs met may have fragile attachment. They do not develop the sense that they are worthy. Children who are not safe remain in survival mode. Their amygdalae are constantly firing, increasing their need to freeze, flee, or fight. They struggle to learn from their mistakes. In their minds, a misspelled word is evidence that they are stupid.

There are strategies that can be employed in the classroom and school wide that will support the development of safety for your lions. It also helps the ducks increase their feeling of well-being. Children need to know that we accept their past, support their present, and encourage their future. The most important strategy for developing safety is language. The use of relationship building language will develop safety in students and will also help your teachers shift their paradigm from a traditional lens to a trauma-informed one.

When you ask someone what is wrong with them, what are you really saying? You are saying that there **_IS_** something wrong with them. Instead of, "What is wrong with you?" ask, "What is going on?" "What is in your way?" Asking children what is in their way or asking how we can help them communicates that we care, that we accept them and removes the feelings of blame and shame.

Instead of _won't_, say _can't._ This small word change shifts our belief system. It helps us believe that students, all people, _would_ complete a task if they _could_. If students are not learning or behaving in a productive way, consider that they would if they could. Assuming can't instead of won't changes the way we approach students. It changes how we communicate with them.

Dr. Sadin tells the story of Louis -

> _Louis was a constant distraction in his math class. His teacher, Mrs. Smith, was frustrated by his lack of assignment completion. Louis rarely engaged in the classroom activities and never did his homework. She came to my office to express her frustration._

Mrs. Smith - *Louis will not do any work in my class. I have repeatedly asked him to complete class assignments. I told him that his grade was below a C because he was not doing his homework. I gave him lunch detention. He did not show. I do not know what is wrong with him. He better start completing work or he will fail this class.*

Dr. Sadin - *What is in his way?*

Mrs. Smith - *I do not know. I know he is capable of understanding the concepts.*

Dr. Sadin - *Ask him what is in his way. Ask him how you can help him. If Louis knows that you are in his corner and want to see him succeed, he might be more willing to engage in your class.*

A week later, Mrs. Smith reported that Louis was making more of an effort in her class. She explained that when she first asked him what was in his way, he said, "Nothing. I hate math." She was persistent. Each day she made another genuine attempt to communicate with him. Finally, he told her that he was really tired. He did not sleep much in his house because his care givers were always fighting. He told her that he was completely lost in math and did not see any way to make his situation better. It was a lost cause. Mrs. Smith reviewed Louis' beginning of the year math test and found that he had a decent foundation but had some gaps in skills that he needed to be successful in her class. She and Louis met after school for a few weeks and filled in the gaps. Louis began to participate in class. His distracting behavior was a thing of the past. He was still tired but was demonstrating an attempt to engage in class. Mrs. Smith and Louis agreed that he would come to her class at the end of the day (while she was preparing for the next day) and complete his homework.

Mrs. Smith built a relationship with Louis by showing him that she cared. He began to feel safe with her. He was more willing to admit when he did not understand something, giving Mrs. Smith the opportunity to help him.

Safety in the School

There are things that school leaders can put in place school wide that will create three-dimensional safety for students. What are the rules in your school? Do the students know them? Are the rules in the hall the same as the rules in the classroom? School and classroom rules should be very similar. Keep the list short. We suggest the following –

1.   Take care of self.
2.   Take care of others.
3.   Take care of stuff.

These rules are appropriate for students in grades pre-K - 12. Usually, anything that happens in a school fits into one of the three rules. If you are using Positive Behavior Intervention and Supports (PBIS), speak with your teachers about condensing the rules. The suggested rules offered by PBIS are aligned with the three rules above. We recommend the development of the rules with the students in the first six weeks of school. The rules that the students suggest can be ascribed to the three rules above. They might be in the words of the students in class, but they will all have the same underlying meaning.

Another consideration in the area of safety is substitute teachers. Many students with fragile attachment struggle with substitutes. Subs are people with whom they do not have a relationship. In addition, subs are often not highly trained educators. They may act or speak in ways that seem threatening to lions. Hiring permanent substitutes is the best solution to this problem. It allows you to provide training and coaching. They are in the school every day and become known by the students. In the absence of funding for permanent subs, consider a plan for your lions who demonstrate the least ability to tolerate substitutes. Is there an alternative space for them for the day or class when there is a sub? Put a plan in place so that everyone, *especially* the student, knows what will happen in the event of a substitute teacher.

Connection

We all need to be connected. It is part of the human condition. We are social animals. Few of us do well completely on our own. Some of us are introverted and prefer time alone with a good book. Some of us are extroverts who prefer time with friends at a party, restaurant, or backyard barbeque. Whether you are an introvert or an extrovert, you still need connection. We find connection in our family, our houses of worship, clubs that we join, even the gym or yoga studio. Children who have fragile attachment and/or who experience trauma find it very difficult to feel connected. Many of the school shooters from the past twenty years had two things in common - they were hurt or suffered loss as children, and they were not connected at school. Most were not behavior problems. They were not participants in any of their high school clubs or sports. They were largely invisible.

Classrooms and schools provide us with excellent opportunities for connection.

Consider this activity –

At a staff meeting ask staff members to write down the names of three students they believe they have a personal connection with and to rank them from strongest to weakest if they could. If not, just three names would be fine. Collect the papers. During your meeting put all students' names on chart paper and place a blue dot next to their name if they were a staff member's first choice, green dot for second choice, and yellow for third choice. As you can imagine, many staff members write down the same names, and lots of students receive an abundance of dots. However, that is not the data we are interested in. There may be a handful of students who did not receive a single dot. Not one. Reach out to these students.

At your next staff meeting share the list of students who were identified as not being connected and ask for volunteers to reach out to each of them.   Let the staff know in the beginning of the meeting that they would not be paired with any student with whom they did not feel they could make a meaningful connection. Support the staff by providing them time to meet with their student.

A similar activity – Connect the Dots

In November, bring the staff together. Review the meaning of connection. Connection is knowing five things about a student outside of his/her academic profile. Remind teachers that they cannot be connected to all of their students. Each teacher is given five dots. Prior to the meeting, create posters with thumbnail photos of each student in your school. The pictures are arranged in rows with plenty of space between them.

The posters are hung on the walls around the room. For a large staff, you can break this down by grade level. The teachers walk around the room placing dots below any student in the school to whom they feel connected. When all the dots have been placed, look around the room. The dots make bar graphs for connection. Find the students with no dots. As a group, discuss who might be willing to make a connection with a particular student. At a follow up faculty meeting, take time to check in on the teachers and their new "friends". Occasionally, a teacher will report that their attempts at connecting are not working with a particular student. Find another staff member to give it a try.

Another activity that is excellent for high schools -

Most schools have a data collection system such as PowerSchool, Genesis, or Frontline. All student data is collected in that system. Most schools keep a record of the students who participate in the many clubs and sports offered to high school students. Run the list of students in clubs and sports against the entire student population. What falls out will be a list of students who do not participate in anything. Find those students. Make a connection. Maybe they can be convinced to participate in a club or have lunch with a mentor. Over time, you will find that there are less students coming out as not connected when you run the list through your data system.

Regulation

When children have overactive amygdala and a heightened stress response system, they need to learn to regulate these systems. Teachers need to learn about the limbic system and explicitly teach it to their students. When students understand why they lose their patience or become angry, they are better able to do something about it.

There are some excellent resources out there to teach about the limbic system and provide suggestions for regulation activities. The *MindUp* curriculum (available from Nathan Levy Books LLC) provides developmentally appropriate lessons for K-2, 3-5, and 6-8 graders.

Regulation in the Classroom

Regulation Space

Create a space in the classroom for children to participate in regulation activities. A chill out space, keep calm corner, or place of peace can be created as needed. This space can be temporary or a permanent place in your classroom. Teach the children to use the space. The regulation space should be a place where children can go to actively work to regain control of their emotions. When children demonstrate the need for regulation, encourage them to consider going there. Keep in mind that this should not turn into the corner of shame where students are sent. Not all students will find the keep calm corner helpful.

Some teachers may notice that one of their students takes up residence in the place of peace. If you know this child has been exposed to trauma, make a plan to increase the time that the student is able to work in the general classroom space. Be patient. Work with the student to increase engagement in classroom activities.

Consider Iggy. Iggy came to kindergarten with a wonderful giggle and very little of anything else. As time went by, his teacher learned that he was living with his grandmother. His father was incarcerated, and his mother was gone. His grandmother loved him. He came to school clean and wearing appropriate clothing. In September, Iggy ran out of the classroom multiple times a week. Usually, when it was time for him to sit and engage in an assignment, he would laugh as he ran circles around the school. Sometimes he would take things off the bulletin boards as he ran by. He never tried to leave the building. His teacher put a plan in place with her principal, counselor and colleagues. When Iggy took off, someone would cover the class, and the teacher would go down the hall and let Iggy know she was there. She did not chase him, and she did not threaten him. She just stood at an intersection of the hallways so he could see her when he ran by. Then she would move down the hall toward her classroom when he was looking at her. He would run past and get to the classroom first or follow not very far behind.

Over time, Iggy would stand in the doorway when he became stressed, but he would not leave. He was becoming attached to his teacher. She became safe to him. Then the teacher set up a keep calm corner. Iggy moved in. He was in the corner all day, but he was not disrupting the class, picking on classmates or running out of the room. Once in a while, he would work one-on-one with the teacher on an assignment. Then, he began participating in class discussions from his corner. The teacher moved his guided reading group to a table next to the corner. Iggy was listening. He ended the school year spending half the day in the corner, and half the day with the class. He was much calmer. He was also on grade level in most academic areas.

Regulation Tools

In addition to a chill out space, all classrooms need to be equipped with regulation tools. Regulation tools can be anything that aids in the regulation of our stress response system. Some tools that have shown to be durable and effective include glitter wands, silicone sponges, fuzzy sticks, and silly putty. Try to include tactile and visual regulation items.

When rolling out the use of regulation tools, keep in mind the following:

- Teachers must have a firm understanding of the reason students benefit from the use of regulation tools.
- Regulation tools are not a reward or consequence.
- Students must be taught about their brain before the roll out of tools.
- Students should be explicitly taught about the tools and how they are to be used.

Regulation in the School

There are a number of ways that school leaders can increase the opportunity for regulation in the school. Some of them you may already have in your building. Others may require some creativity on your part regarding time and money.

The Expanded Role of the OT

Do you have an occupational therapist? They are typically pre-wired for trauma-informed care based on their pre-service training. A one-day workshop or the reading of the book, The Body Keeps the Score by Bessel van der Kolk, is often all they need to be on board as a resource. Set up the occupational therapy room as a space that is available to general education students as well as children with IEPs. Most occupational therapists already have the tools they need to assist children in getting regulated. Consider applying for a grant to enhance the equipment in the space. This is a great use of grant money since the funding does not need to be ongoing.

Tap In / Tap Out

This is a regulation opportunity for your staff. As they become more aware of their own triggers and regulation needs, they will take advantage of the opportunity to take a minute to collect themselves. Take a good look at the faculty room. Is the copy machine in there? Take it out. Make the faculty room a place that is welcoming and relaxing. Create a keep calm space for the adults in the building. Include a water feature and comfortable seating. In one school, the science teacher took the responsibility for a beautiful saltwater fish tank in the faculty room. Consider the lighting. Can you reduce the overhead fluorescent lighting and add floor to table lamps?

The tap in/tap out program has a number of benefits. The first thing you may notice is improvement in faculty attendance. Research shows that schools that provide care for the adults have better overall attendance. Teachers have commented that they used it as an opportunity to access the restroom at more convenient times. Teachers will drink more water and boost their immune systems if they do not have to wait three hours to use the restroom. Another benefit you may notice is an overall improvement in people's attitudes toward each other and the students. Adults who can take care of their emotional needs are better prepared to assist others with their emotional needs.

Take a Sensory Audit

Walk through your school. Take note of what you hear, smell, see, touch. We will leave taste out of the sensory audit of a school.

What do you see?
Are the hallways neat and clean? Are there some things on the wall? Too little student work and the school can seem cold. Too much work on the walls can be over stimulating. The same is true in classrooms. Make sure the teachers put on the wall what is relevant to instruction. Rotate anchor charts. Use the things on the wall for instruction. Allow for bare spaces.

What do you hear?
If you work in middle or high school, you probably hear bells signaling the passing of classes. Consider music to signal the end of a class period. Avoid music with lyrics. Soft rock, classical, and recording of instruments played by the sea are all good for our brains. There are free recordings of "singing bowls" on YouTube that are great for this. Chimes work as well. Using soft music to signal class times may improve behavior in the halls. The hallways may be quieter when students are passing.

What do you touch?

Are there hard and soft seating opportunities? Consider including a basket of markers and coloring in the office where care givers wait for students. Include regulation tools in the basket. A sign of invitation and explanation will inform care givers as well as calm them.

Consider the cafeteria.

The cafeteria may be the biggest challenge when seeking to create calming environments within our school. Schools must feed a very large group of children in a very short amount of time. Students with early childhood trauma suffer in a large unstructured setting such as the lunchroom for a number of reasons. They sometimes fail to recognize non-verbal cues so the lunchroom can be a torture chamber of misunderstood peer interactions. The smells, sounds, and close human contact can be over stimulating or triggering to a brain that is already running on high alert.

A water feature (changing colors and bubbles behind Plexiglas) on the wall may serve to reduce noise. Small group seating and appropriate ceiling tile also serve to reduce overall noise. For some students, even these efforts will not make the cafeteria a place that is conducive to appropriate engagement with peers. Create an alternative setting to the cafeteria. Depending on the size of your school, a conference room or media center might work. Assign a lunch aide to the alternative space. Allow students to choose to eat in the alternative space. Some students will use it occasionally. Some students will eat there every day. In our trainings, we are sometimes asked if allowing a student to avoid the cafeteria indefinitely is helping the students prepare for the "real world". We offer the following two responses - (1) Students with peanut allergies do not need to eat peanuts to be prepared for the "real world" where others may eat peanuts. Children with peanut allergies need to avoid peanuts forever. Yet they somehow manage to have fulfilled and productive adult lives. (2) What part of the cafeteria is the "real world"? How many adults do you know that eat in a setting like a school cafeteria? The answer is none, if they can help it. There is one place where adults can be found eating in a cafeteria. Prison. That is not the "real world". Helping students understand what works and does not work for them is a far better preparation for the "real world" than a lunchroom. One size fits one in instructional settings and in non-instructional settings.

> **NOTE -** Avoid sending students to the alternative lunchroom as a punishment for a problem in the lunchroom. Remember this is a teachable moment. This is where whole school understanding of brain development helps. Explain that the lunchroom might be a trigger for the student. Encourage them to use the alternative lunch space until they have created a plan for success in the larger cafeteria.

LEARN!

Trauma-informed instruction is superior instruction. Think about it. Many school leaders can identify the one or few teachers in their school who never send their students to the office. They rarely complete discipline referrals. We call them Kid Whisperers. Dr. Sadin remembers a teacher she worked with in an elementary school.

> *I had been working with a young boy for the previous 3 years. He was in and out of class. In and out of my office. In and out of the*

counselor's office. Nothing we tried worked for any length of time. (Oh if I had known then what I know now.....). I placed him in the class with the teacher who never removed students. Sure enough. I saw the student only in passing in the hall that year. At the end of the year, his grades were proficient. His formative assessments indicated that he learned the curriculum for that year. His attendance was good. The following year, he was back in my office by the middle of September.

According to Dr. Sadin's observation, one of our authors, Nathan Levy, was the epitome of a "kid whisperer" as an inner city teacher, a principal of two elementary schools, the principal of a 1200 pupil district wide grade 5-6 school and as a consultant to school districts all over the world. Nathan has had great vision in helping traumatized and all other children. As a teacher, Nathan Levy helped kids who had all kinds of discipline issues become learners. As a principal of two schools with "troubled kids," the children were able to be consistently productive. The difficult kids from seven elementary schools that entered into

Nathan's district wide school "disappeared as problems" for their two years in that school. Nathan used the trauma informed strategies we recommend before he even knew the name "trauma informed." As he continued to learn, he was able to aid other school leaders who went from teacher to principal/assistant principal and several to the role of superintendent (there are about twenty of them) as well as students in his districts.

Building on student interests and strengths and then training teachers on strategies to make connections to the desired curriculum are keys to helping ducks and lions make the desired progress. It also helps children with trauma make the gains that foster growth and positive self-confidence.

What do kid whisperers do that other teachers do not? They lead with compassion and consistently provide differentiated, challenging, and engaging lessons. Trauma-informed teaching is superior teaching. Schools, however, are full of teachers with varying teaching abilities and training.

Think of your trauma-informed schools process the same way you think about the roll out of a new reading program. The key to successful implementation is thorough training of the staff and a plan for ongoing support.

Consider the Curriculum

As you move through your curriculum review cycle, look for activities that might presume a life without ACEs. In elementary school, are you having a Mother's Day tea? Are all of the students making Mother's Day cards? What if a child lives with a foster parent? What if a child is adopted? What if a child lives with a mother who is neglecting or harming him? Avoid family specific activities. When your third or fourth grade curriculum gets to the unit on culture, allow children to select a culture from a list. This allows children to select their own or one they are interested in. Children who are adopted can select their country of origin.....or not. Children who live in homes where discussions of the family tree do not occur or are wrought with sorrow can pick something less triggering.

Since we cannot know all of the ACEs a child lives with, it is best to err on the side of caution. Curriculum directors and committees should be trained in ACEs so they can look through a trauma-informed lens when they review curriculum. A good rule of thumb assumes all the children in your school have ten ACEs and go from there.

The Role of Executive Function

Intelligence is considered to be the capacity to learn from experience using metacognitive processes to enhance learning and the ability to adapt to the surrounding environment. Metacognitive in this case means the ability to think about thinking. It is a completely cognitive function requiring pre-frontal cortex activity. In addition, the ability to adapt to one's surroundings indicates intelligence. If you compare the ability of an eighth grader without trauma to think about thinking and to adapt to his surroundings with the ability of an eighth grader with trauma, it is likely that the eighth grader with trauma would come up lacking.

Our brain development cannot skip stages. If a child does not get sufficient opportunity for attachment and care in the early years, development in the hippocampus and pre-frontal cortex can be stalled. Therefore, an eighth [h] grader with a trauma history may have the metacognitive ability of a fifth grader because that is his/her current level of brain development.

Trauma-informed education is creating opportunities in school for brain development. This can be done by employing all of the strategies already covered in this book such as self-regulation, creating a feeling of safety, establishing trusting relationships, and teaching your students to think.

Executive functions are the skills required to conspire together to create metacognition, skills including auditory processing, memory, planning, language processing, logic and reasoning, visual processing, and comprehension. These skills are needed to assist students in everything we ask them to do in school. They need memory to follow two-step directions and to retain new content. They need planning to organize their learning material and to plan their approach to a task.

They need attention to focus on a task and to persevere through a task. They need logic and reasoning to know what to ask when they do not understand.

Provide training for your teachers on the development of executive function. Students who are explicitly taught executive function skills usually perform better across all levels of academic ability.

4

Self-Care

Your role as a school leader is to take care of the adult ducks and lions the same way you want your staff to take care of the student ducks and lions. Our four R's framework applies to self-care as well as it applies to the school.

Mr. Rothacker shares -

As I work with schools across the country, I always pose the same question to the participants: "Why did you choose the field of education?" We know it is not because of the salary or the public recognition, so why did you choose to be in a field that is so demanding? The answer always boils down to the same thing, "It is in my heart to help others." I know that feeling first hand. After 11 years as a teacher, I left the profession to strike it rich as an Education Computer Consultant for a well-known computer company. I would sell computers to schools and then conduct on-site trainings. I soon realized that my heart was still in the classroom and six months later I returned to teaching. After thirty three years, I retired from the public-school system in July of 2013. However, in September of the same year I was doing administrative interim work. In September of 2015, I became the Director of Education for an alternative school for adolescent girls who have been placed by the courts because of the behavioral challenges they have presented in their home school and community. THIS is where my heart is.

It takes a very special person to be a superior educator. There is something in their genetic fabric that provides them with the fortitude and courage to persevere each day. Being an effective teacher is becoming more and more challenging. And, because educators inherently put the needs of others over their own, they somehow juggle the burdens of running a household, managing their own children, and meeting the needs of their students. All of this translates into a great formula for emotional burnout.

Consider vicarious trauma and compassion fatigue. Both are prevalent in our schools. Vicarious trauma occurs with constant exposure to people who are experiencing trauma. Educators who work in schools that are in settings where there is ongoing military conflict or neighborhood violence will experience vicarious trauma. In this type of trauma, the traumatic events are ongoing and pervasive.

Compassion fatigue (as defined by the Webster Dictionary, 2019) is the physical and mental exhaustion and emotional withdrawal experienced by those who care for sick or traumatized people over an extended period of time. This is the result of caring deeply for and about children who are suffering.

Trauma sensitive school leaders must create opportunities to care for the adults in their school. Adult survivors of trauma will often have a stronger physical or emotional response to vicarious trauma or compassion fatigue due to their overworked stress response system. Teach your staff about ACEs so they understand how to care for themselves based on their own childhood trauma exposure. Respond to all of your staff as if they are traumatized children...with compassion and acceptance. Ask, "What is in your way?" or "How can I help you?" rather than, "What is wrong with you?"

Realize the Prevalence of Trauma

The statistics regarding exposure to adverse childhood experiences are the same for the adults in your school as for your students. It is safe to assume that several of the adults in your school are lions. Teach the adults in your school community about ACEs. Give the survey so they know their ACE score. Talk to them about how self-care can improve their health and their ability to do their job.

Recognize the Impact of Trauma on Learning and Behavior

Just as we discussed in the previous chapter, the childhood experiences of the staff in your school will impact their learning and their behavior.   Some of your teachers are high functioning lions because they achieved certification and college degrees. But they are lions, nonetheless. The impact of their ACEs might be seen in their interaction with students. Are they quick to anger? Do they sometimes seem afraid of the volatile students? Consider their interactions with their colleagues and think about what you now know about attachment. The adult lions in your school may have fragile attachment. They may be awkward with other adults. Sometimes, adults with fragile attachment are hesitant to connect with students. They may express an unwillingness to be an attachment figure for their students. This comes from their fear of being rejected.

Respond in a Trauma-Informed Way

One efficient method to have staff treat students in a trauma informed manner is to have staff experience what it feels like to be treated in a trauma-informed way. You must start with the perspective that they are doing the best they can under the conditions, just as we want them to do with their students. It feels good. It makes people feel valued and appreciated. It also gives them the license to admit that they cannot be all things to all people all the time. Administrators need to demonstrate genuine caring for their staff members. This is not about celebration. It is about appreciation. You need to find a way for staff members to be able to "tap out" when the stress becomes overwhelming. This will be hard for them to admit at first. However, trauma controlled brains are not positioned to learn OR to teach.

Remember to take care of YOURSELF! Lead by example. Have regulation tools on your desk or in your office. Use them. We added coloring pages to this book so you can take some time for yourself in the middle of reading.

5

The 4th R – Resist Traumatization

Resist traumatization means avoid making things worse for your students and your staff. This is an ongoing process that can take years. The more you and your staff respond in a trauma-informed way, the less likely you are to traumatize your students. As the classrooms become trauma-informed, so too must the hallways and the principal's office. Resisting traumatization involves a whole school approach to your students. Before you go about changing school wide practices and district policy, however, we suggest you take a minute to understand how we came to be where we are with school discipline and prepare ourselves for a bit of a paradigm shift. Remember, if we keep doing what we have always done, we will keep getting what we have always gotten.

The School to Prison Pipeline

The school to prison pipeline is a phrase that refers to the statistical evidence that children who are suspended are more likely to be involved with the juvenile or adult justice system. The school to prison pipeline grew out of the country's collective response to the shooting at Columbine High School. That was the beginning of our understanding that our schools might not be as safe as we thought they were. Our government responded with a national call for zero tolerance. School policy was written. The spirit of zero tolerance policy was that schools were safe places for children who wanted to learn. If a student demonstrated unsafe behavior or brought weapons and/or drugs to school, they could be removed from the school. Teachers were scared. Care givers wanted assurances that their children were safe in school. School leaders wanted policy they could use to help create safe schools.

Over time, however, in some places more than others, the zero tolerance policies led to more and more school suspensions. Children were being expelled in record numbers. Some district leaders expanded the zero tolerance policies to include repeat behaviors such as cursing or disrespect toward teachers. A few years after the nationwide implementation of zero tolerance, researchers began to look at the impact of these practices on students. What they found was that black, Hispanic, and special education male students were being suspended much more often than their non-minority and general education classmates. This practice is now referred to as disproportionality. Many states have administrative code that attempts to thwart the practice of disproportionately suspending minority and special education students through careful reporting of discipline records. It is a start. We have a long way to go.

In addition, the research showed that minority students were suspended for non-violent behaviors where non-minority students demonstrating the same behavior were only reprimanded (Scuba, 2014). Longitudinal study showed that children who were suspended once in their freshman year were more likely to be suspended again. In addition, children who were suspended were more likely to have poor attendance. They were more likely to fail a class and a grade. They were more likely to drop out.

An in-depth review of the literature regarding the school to prison pipeline along with consideration of children with adverse childhood experiences in our schools expands disproportionality to include children with early childhood trauma. A review of school data in Washington State showed that children with three or more ACEs were more likely to receive special education and fail a grade. They were more likely to have poor attendance and more likely to drop out than their classmates with no ACEs. The children in the school to prison pipeline ARE the children with early childhood trauma. School policy is causing school leaders to suspend the lions much more frequently than they suspend the ducks. These are the children who have, most likely, already been emotionally abandoned by their care givers or their communities. They are the children with fragile attachment. They are the last children we should be sending away from our care and protection. Trauma-informed schools are schools where children are only suspended for extremely dangerous behavior or for bringing weapons and guns to school. It is important to note that the authors are familiar with schools where children who need to be removed for weapons or drugs remain connected to the school through contact with a guidance counselor, teacher, or administrator. Sometimes students need more than we can provide in a school. Sometimes they need a therapeutic environment or a drug treatment program. In those cases, we strongly recommend that you find a way to stay connected. Communicate that you still care and that you look forward to having the student return to school when s/he is well.

So now what? Take away detention and suspension and do what? First consider the paradigm shift. Take a minute to reflect on your beliefs about crime and punishment and about the concept of fair.

Crime and Punishment

Punishment does not work for all children. Responding to behavior works for all children. We want our students to grow and learn. We want them to leave our schools prepared for the next chapter in their lives. We want them to be productive and content citizens. We need to teach them, not punish them. In the United States, if you break a law, you are punished. Punishment can be anything from a fine to time in prison. Historically, this system was created based on the understanding that if a person broke a law and went to prison, that might deter someone else from doing it. In the United States, this practice can be traced back to colonial times. Those who broke the law were put in the stockade for all in the town to see what would happen to people who broke the law. If this concept of deterrent worked, there would be a lot less people currently sitting in prison.

A quote that we recently saw.
"No punishment has ever possessed enough power of deterrence to prevent the commission of crimes."
Hannah Arendt, quoted in Lapham's Quarterly.

Another contributing belief to our concept of crime and punishment is that if we do not punish bad behavior, the behavior will be repeated. Dr. Sadin recalls her talented, beautiful mother, who was also a lifelong educator, telling her as a child, "Melissa, if I don't punish you, you will do this again. It is for your own good." Most of the time, Melissa did it again. How many of the students in your school who have been assigned discipline were assigned discipline again? Dr. Sadin has done the research. For 80% of you the answer is most, if not all of the students who were assigned punishment, were assigned the same or another punishment. If punishment worked perfectly, this would not be the case.

Fair is Not Always Fair

You are sitting in your doctor's reception area waiting to be seen for the horrible upper respiratory cold you have been battling for over a week now. To your immediate left is an older gentleman who appears to be suffering from an infected finger. Across from you sits an elderly woman who appears to be in a lot of discomfort claiming that the pain medicine the doctor prescribed for her arthritis last week is not working. Finally, a young man enters the reception area holding a cloth over his eye stating that he was cutting wood and he believes there is a sliver caught under his eyelid.

Now imagine the reaction from those people if the doctor entered the reception area and stated, "There's no need to see each of you individually. I will give everyone a prescription for citalopram (an antidepressant)."

As ludicrous as that sounds, many people believe that in order to be fair, we need to treat everyone the same. If Billy gets it then Kierra deserves it, and if I do it for Sally, I must do it for Jovan as well. Nothing could be farther from the truth when it comes to fairness. <u>Treating students fairly is giving each student what they need, and that is going to vary from child to child</u>. One size fits one. Thomas Jefferson got it right. "There is nothing more **unequal** then the **equal treatment of unequal** people"

It is fair to say that, as educators, we must position ourselves to be willing to treat students differently. And to do so, we must consider all factors (including ACEs) when determining the correct course of action when decisions about inappropriate student behavior are made. As Dr. Sadin says so succinctly, "One size fits one."

The Reading Revelation

Consider the teaching of reading. When we provide workshops for teachers, we sometimes ask them, "Can you please raise your hand if you think it is not important to teach reading?" No one ever does. The same response is provided in groups of early childhood teachers and groups of middle and high school teachers. All teachers know that learning to read impacts the learning of all other content. All teachers, in their own way, are involved in the teaching of reading. Some teachers teach reading for the sake of reading. Others use the ability to read to deliver their subject area content. All educators understand and support the development of reading skills.

Now we ask you, the school leaders, "Can you please raise your hand if you have ever punished a child for not being able to read a word or passage?" We cannot see you, but we are going to go ahead with the understanding that none of you raised your hands.

Some of our students make continuous progress in reading. They make adequate yearly progress thorough our curriculum. Others require some type of Tier 2 or Tier 3 intervention. Some need a more phonics-based instruction. In the United States, we have some of the best reading intervention programs in the world. Teachers and administrators work tirelessly to help all of our students learn to read whether that takes one year or five years.

We need to see behavior as a learned skill like reading. Some of our students never need direct instruction in their social and emotional development. Others need some assistance from our teachers and school counselors.

Children with fragile attachment who may be largely amygdala driven even into their teens, need specific and explicit instruction in forming relationships and regulating their behavior. When a child struggles to read, we help the child. In the absence of harm to others and self, when a child throws a book at a wall, we blame the child. A trauma-informed response to a child who throws the book should be the same as a child who mispronounces or omits a word when reading. We want to get across the message, "What is in your way?" How can I help you?" Our response to the student needs to have an instructional tone, not a punitive one. We do not say, "If you read that word incorrectly one more time, I will give you detention." So why would we say, "If you throw that object one more time, I will give you detention"? When a child struggles to read, we provide interventions. When a child struggles to behave in a safe and productive way, we need to provide intervention, not detention.

From Discipline to Behavior Response

Trauma-informed schools are not schools where the students are permitted to run wild and where no one is held accountable. Quite the opposite. There is an immediate and appropriate response given to a student in a trauma-informed school who demonstrates unsafe behavior or who becomes dysregulated.

The reading revelation shows us that we need to move from punishment to behavior response. Punishment very often does not work (See Crime and Punishment above). Behavior response can be treated like a reading intervention. Collect baseline data. Apply an intervention or support. Measure progress. After six to eight weeks, review the progress or lack thereof. Many know this as the Response to Intervention framework (RTI). It is also the basis of Positive Intervention and Behavioral Supports (PBIS).

One of the main strategies of a trauma sensitive school is to bring students and staff closer together by creating deeper and genuine relationships among them. Understanding the effects of ACEs should lead educators towards a more empathic teaching style, which, in turn, should translate into more connectivity between teachers and students. We must continue to find ways to close the emotional gaps between teachers and their students.

Keep in mind that people with a history of trauma are often led to believe that they have little to offer the world, and they are the ones to blame for their disturbing past. They are guilt ridden and full of shame.

Suspensions from classroom instruction widen the gap between the adults and students, and also reinforce the student's belief of, "I am no good anyway." And, keeping students out of the classroom puts them further behind academically creating greater probability of behavioral and academic difficulty in the future. Our message should be that being in class is very important because this is where the learning takes place.

The plan to rectify the situation should be swift and deliberate. Fix what you broke, learn from your actions, and create an alternate plan if this situation arises again. That is the message. The most important things to mend are the relationships that were strained or damaged during the inappropriate behavior. If these are not addressed, no progress will be made and future similar episodes can be predicted.

The shift from punishment to behavior response requires a shift from our typical strategies, which are largely reactive, to a more proactive approach. Physical safety must be our first priority. We must respond immediately to a child who has a weapon, is carrying drugs, or who is under the influence of a controlled or illegal substance. In the case of weapons, we must involve law enforcement officials. In the case of substance abuse, a student may need medical or crisis intervention. We need to respond to these behaviors, but we can maintain relationships and connection. There have been times when Mr. Rothacker has ridden in the ambulance with one of his students who was having an emotional breakdown. Dr. Sadin has spent hours in crisis centers with students and their care givers. The message is, "We must keep you and everyone else in the school safe, but we still care about you."

In addition to these unfortunate situations that require a reaction, school leaders should consider building proactive practices and programs. Programs described below, and all of the strategies in the "Respond" chapter will reduce the number of children who require a reaction.

Behavior Response

Every time we work in a school or speak with trauma-informed educators, we learn about another fantastic behavior response. Some that we have seen in action and can verify effectiveness include –

1. **The Walk and Talk** (Katherine Cosby from Middleton Elementary School in Middleton, NH) – one of the single greatest regulation activities is walking. It supports students who are angry. It supports students who are sad or sleepy. Students who need a walk need supervision. Build it into your duty schedule. Teachers love this duty! They hold a radio, or you can use a cell phone. They can work on grading papers, making copies, anything, until they are summoned. Then they pick up the student and start walking. Going outside is highly recommended, weather permitting. It is important to teach your walk and talk staff that they do not need to solve the student's

problems. Nor does a student have to talk. If a student shares and uses inappropriate language, let it go. Walk and Talk staff need only to let the student know they are listening.

2. **The Monarch Room or AIR Time**- The Monarch Room because students enter the room in one emotional state and exit in another. AIR Time stands for "Alternate Intervention Room" Time.

    This is nothing more than a retrofitted in-school suspension room. Create a permanent space. Add a water feature. Provide a couch and a few bean bag chairs, perhaps a rug. Sometimes students need to come out of the general population to work through a problem. Sometimes students need to come out of the general population to give the *other* students a break. Use the time in this space in full support of the student. They should get time with their favorite people. Hopefully, one of those is the school psychologist or counselor. Teachers can use this time to help students get caught up on work. Coverage of the teacher's class can be provided so that s/he can spend a few hours working one-on-one with the student in AIR time. To the people who are concerned that all the students will demonstrate unsafe behavior so that they can go to the Monarch room, we say – that simply does not happen. In one location where Dr. Sadin was working, there was a slight uptick in dysregulated behavior demonstrated by a few "repeat offenders" for a few days. Then it tapered off. Remember from our attachment chapter, children who do not get what they need struggle to make connections and establish relationships. Some of our students are amygdala driven and struggle to feel safe. These two facets of development are the reason why we need to lean into our students who struggle with behavior regulation. They need more of us, not less.

3. **Alternative Lunch - As discussed in Chapter 4 Flipped Bathrooms (Dr. Rogo, Neptune Middle School, Neptune, NJ)** – The bathroom can be a very dangerous place for our students. For starters, everything in there is hard. There is no soft place to land. Add water and a total lack of adult supervision, and you have a recipe for disaster. In some schools, particularly in middle and high schools, the bathroom can be a place where children are bullied, access illegal substances, or get recruited into gangs. Rather than spend half you day punishing kids for inappropriate behavior in the bathroom and asking teachers to create time consuming and ineffective sign-out logs, consider flipping the bathrooms. Lock all of the student bathrooms and provide a key to your staff. Give the staff bathrooms to the students. They are smaller and, in some cases, individual spaces. Students then use the bathroom one at a time. It also helps if you

need a gender-neutral bathroom for your transgender or non-binary students.

We are confident that you will find many of your own behavior responses that are good for all and fit your students' needs. Take a look at spaces that are historically troubling. If Billy always has a problem in the lunchroom, take him out of the lunchroom. Explain why. Occasionally you will have a student who, despite a problem fighting or crying every day in the cafeteria, does not want to access the alternative lunch space. You may occasionally find a student using illegal substances in the flipped bathroom. A trauma-informed behavior response approach does not mean that you will never have a student struggle with his/her behavior. It will, however, greatly reduce the frequency of these occurrences.

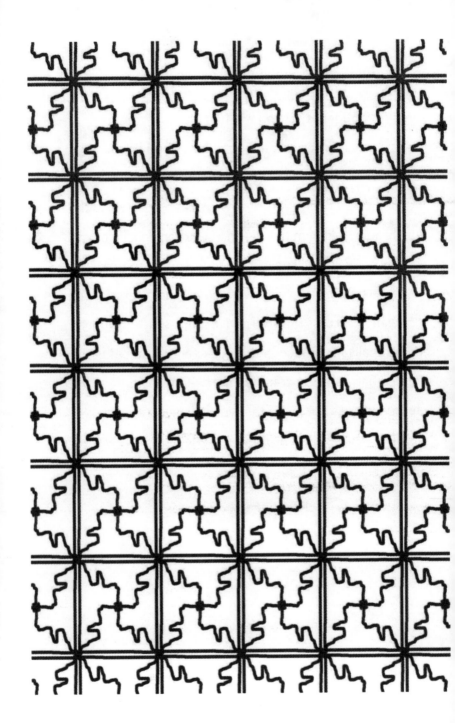

6

Whole School Change – A Systematic Approach

Early indications from research show clearly that changes at the school and district level must take place for a school to find success in becoming trauma informed. Like Social Emotional Learning (SEL), this type of climate change should involve everyone, or it may not be sustainable. More importantly, our work with schools around the country has shown us that, while every school district is unique, there are characteristics of whole school reform that are successful in most situations. Our approach follows the steps of exemplary professional development and effective systems change.

As a strong leader and advocate for your students, you will be excited and eager to begin improving your school to be founded on trauma sensitivity. It is critically important to keep in mind that your school is part of a larger entity, the school district. It is unrealistic to assume that all stakeholders will share the same level of passion for the paradigm shifts associated with a trauma sensitive school. The last thing a superintendent wants or deserves is to be blindsided (particularly publicly) by someone who has questions, and you have not informed him/her of your leadership intentions to move in a Trauma Sensitive School (TSS) direction, and therefore he/she has no logical answers to the questions posed. As a first priority, we would recommend you set up a private meeting with whomever you identify as the most logical to inform. Share with them your logic for moving in this direction and your tentative plan for implementation. We suggest a private meeting because, at this stage, you too have many unanswered questions and you need time to work them out.

We suggest that once you have the support of the upper leadership echelon, you are ready to establish a small school-based guiding coalition. It is important, but not essential, to ask for volunteers. This will help to ensure that the membership is not perceived as your hand-picked favorites, and you will know that their willingness to participate is genuine. We strongly suggest that you make sure the membership is balanced between enthusiastic go-getters and detail-oriented workers. If a strong union is a factor, it would be wise to include someone from that leadership group as well (maybe even as a co-facilitator of the group). Although this blended membership will most likely slow down the initial process, it will undoubtedly expedite things in the long run, and the coalition will address any issues upfront and behind closed doors. It is up to you as to whether or not you should be a member of this group. You know the culture of your building the best. Some administrators choose to not be on the team to allow for more open dialog during meetings, others do not feel the need to stay away. Either way, it is important to establish upfront what the role of the committee is going to be. Is it going to be an advisory group with no decision-making authority? Or, is it *the* decision-making body? This needs to be very clear from the start.

Finally, once the group is established, treat them well. Use staff development funds to get them release time from their duties and buy them lunch so they can delve fully into the Trauma Sensitive School endeavor. People do their best work when they feel valued and important.

Boulders

Change is inevitable, only growth is optional. It is safe to say that you cannot have progress without change. Yet, we know that change is difficult for many. Although we may not be totally satisfied in our current situation, many times we are hesitant to take the risk of making adaptations and modifications towards perceived improvements. Also, change can be hard work and some just do not have the steam to take on one more endeavor. Sadly, education has earned a reputation of continual change without much growth. "Been there done that," and "Just wait it out and it too will change," are two common streams of thought. But, transforming your school is different. It is an attitude and culture that should extend far beyond the school setting. It should be a way of life for all of us. It is work that MUST be done, and the time is long overdue.

You will undoubtedly come across people who are resistant to change. We refer to them as boulders. We like to compare any initiatives for change to the development of a river. The river starts out as a small, weak stream. It has little momentum to clear anything in its path, so it is forced to meander and find a way around obstacles. Additionally, it has no cutting power to create a stable path at this point. Over time, as the volume of the water intensifies, the stream gains power and has the ability to straighten its path by having the capacity and momentum to move those obstacles that were previously stationery. It can now cut deeper and claim its territory.

There is no question that you will come across boulders during your journey of transformation. Do not expend all of your energy trying to move the boulders. Focus on those who are ready to begin the challenge. You know who they are, the movers and shakers in your school. The boulders will eventually be swept up by the momentum and will either join the flow or will be forced to the river bank. Either way, the path has been cleared.

Gap Analysis

Before you can make any changes, you should have a thorough understanding of what you have and what you want. An excellent activity to identify what you have, we call Rocks, Rubies, & Diamonds. Draw a chart with three columns. Use the headings. Rocks, Rubies, and Diamonds. The participants discuss their school and list the things that can be identified in each column. Things can be programs, curriculum, people (no names, please), facilities, professional development, financial, etc. Nothing is off limits. It is ok to put items in more than one category. If one participant thinks the reading intervention program is a rock and another feels it is a ruby, then it goes in both places.

> ROCKS – Things that do not work, are in your way, are out dated, etc.
>
> RUBIES – Things that are good, but not great. They might need some work but are worth keeping. Maybe things that were once great and have lost their polish.
>
> DIAMONDS – Things that you are most proud of. Things that are documented as highly successful/effective.

To find what you want, take time to do a visioning activity. We use Blue Sky, but there are many good ones. The Blue Sky activity is a simple visioning activity. Each participant or small group gets a worksheet. On the worksheet, they describe their dream school or in this case trauma-informed school. Remind them to include the things you would see, hear, and feel in your trauma-informed school.

Put the Rocks, Rubies and the Blue-Sky chart pages side-by-side. Are there any items on both charts? It is common to find that the items in the Diamonds column are in some way connected to things on the Blue-Sky chart.

From Practice to Policy

It is What is in Print that Matters

We caution you about an area that is often overlooked during transformation to a trauma sensitive school. As your enthusiasm and momentum begin to grow, and you are utilizing more and more restorative practices instead of traditional punishments, there will come a time when someone will refer to the Code of Conduct or the District's Policy Manual to challenge your decisions. And, it is what is in print that matters.

Many schools continue to have black and white policies and codes of conduct (if "A" then "B" decision making). However, as we know, the world and our schools exhibit a rainbow of colors and cannot be condensed to such simple thinking, especially in a trauma sensitive school. Remember, our goal is to have students feel safe, connected and valued as individuals. If we continue to treat our students as just another member of the masses, our message will be received as hypocritical and hollow.

With that said, it is critically important that what is in print supports your mission statement and leaves room for administrators to make data informed decisions on a case-by-case basis. Then, and only then, can we begin to treat students fairly.

School Board Policy Change

In the beginning of this chapter, we explained that there is no way to truly become a trauma-informed school without whole school change. We remind you here that this includes district policy. Many of the policies in our extensive policy manuals do not need any attention. Policy regarding material disposal, facilities management, etc. is generally left out of the trauma-informed review. Look carefully, however, at the dress code, conduct codes, and anything else directly related to the students.

Look at the language of the policy. Any "if/then" language should be removed. A good rule of thumb is one size fits one. Language like – "Consider individual circumstances" allows building administrators and restorative teams to provide action that is best for the student. Also, words like "developmental age of the student" are a nod to the slow development of the limbic system for children with childhood trauma exposure.

There are some excellent models of trauma-informed school policy on the internet. Below is a sample of policy Dr. Sadin crafted with the Somerville Board of Education.

The Board of Education approves the use of comprehensive behavioral supports that promote positive student development and the students' abilities to fulfill the behavioral expectations established by the Board. These behavioral supports include, but are not limited to, positive reinforcement for good conduct and academic success including the programs that honor and reward student conduct and academic achievement; supportive intervention and referral services including those services outlined in Policy 2417; remediation of problem behaviors that take into account the behavior's nature, **the students' developmental** ages and the students' histories of problem behaviors and performance; and for students with disabilities, the behavior interventions and supports shall be determined and provided pursuant to N.J.A.C. 6A:14.

The Data

Opinions Do Not Matter

We have all heard the term "data driven." So much so that we may be exhausted by it. A good statistician can manipulate silos of data to support any argument. However, "data informed" decision making certainly has its merits. Looking at data over time to identify trends and patterns will help to decrease the influence of temporary variables that have the potential to skew the results. If you do not collect this longitudinal data to support the initiative, all you will have are people with varying opinions, and opinions do not get it done.

Before you can begin to aggregate and disaggregate data, you first need to decide what it is that you are going to measure to reflect the impact of the changes associated with moving to a trauma sensitive learning environment. This will be different for each school so it is not appropriate for me to tell you what they should be. In Ralph's school, the Guiding Coalition decided to collect and analyze data in four areas:

1. Percent of students with overall passing averages each quarter
2. Mean average each quarter
3. Percent of student passing each New York State Regents Exam
4. Number of critical behavior incidents reported each month

The next step was for the team to go as far back into the data as we could. For our school, that was two years back. We are in our fifth year as a trauma sensitive school, so we have six years of valid data to work with. Without going into specific detail, our results are remarkable. I use this data to help others see the advantages of becoming a trauma sensitive school. Boards of Education and care givers will be asking for "proof". Now you have it. However, more importantly there will be times, days, maybe weeks when things are not going as smoothly as planned and discouragement sets in. This is to be expected but reviewing the longitudinal data and seeing the positive trends will help you to support your staff through this temporary downswing.

So, without data you are just another person with an opinion. Do not be that person, and do not get sucked into data driven decision making. Use the data as a springboard into deeper conversations about the trends it is presenting. Be open-minded and continue to seek meaning in the numbers. Finally, after you have translated the numbers into meaningful conversation, develop action steps to reflect your conversations.

Three Bridges

Mr. Rothacker has said that someone has to cross three bridges before he could be viewed as an expert. Metaphorically speaking, what he means is that it is very difficult to be a prophet in your own land. His thinking is that you need to cross the first bridge out of your school, then cross the second bridge leading out of your district, and finally cross that third bridge taking you to new territories. Then you can confidently present yourself as an "expert" and be seen as such by most audiences. As leaders, we have all experienced this. Mr. Rothacker's staff views him through a different lens than the people he trains across the country.

Recognizing this phenomenon, it is important that you partner with another person or organization that will be viewed as expert. For Mr. Rothacker, it was The Attachment and Trauma Network (ATN). He took over the school at Saint Anne Institute in September of 2015, and by mid-October, Dr. Sadin and her team spent the day with the staff. They learned together, and they became inspired and motivated to begin the journey towards becoming a trauma sensitive school.

He would not have been able to move his school in the manner he did without an expert coming to help kick start the initiative. Even if he knew then what he knows now, it would not have been the same. However, because they learned from the Attachment and Trauma Network, Mr. Rothacker was able to continue to fuel the fire set by them. The staff created a new and improved trauma informed Mission Statement. They are on their way.

Notes about Paradigm Shifting

In order to begin to see change, we must start with the adults within our schools or organization. We must make the shift to look at and treat our students differently. In order to do this, we must first make the change within our own minds. We must continually remind ourselves through our words and our actions that relationships are the center post of a trauma-based school's framework.

Ask most educators what they teach, and a typical response might be, "I teach third grade," or "I teach physics." This is where we need to help ourselves (and each other) make that mental shift. Instead of saying what grade level or subject you teach, we should all give a universal response of, "I teach students" or "I teach people." This simple change to a very commonly asked question will help to remind educators and non-educators that our job is to develop knowledge in others through meaningful relationships. It is not simply to impart information and leave it up to the learner to absorb it or not. Additionally, our new answer helps to solidify our core belief that effective teaching and learning are done best through positive human relationships.

An easy way to begin this discussion with your faculty is to ask them to respond to the following statement: "I taught them, but they did not learn." Most will agree that you did not teach them if they did not learn. From there you can begin to have them develop their own definition of effective teaching, and, more importantly, how you measure it. Having this developed by them instead of you is an important step. It is difficult to argue with yourself. Finally, ask them to list the conditions that educators (not students or care givers)) must create to optimize learning. Hopefully, the discussion will come full circle back to making sure students feel safe, connected and ready to learn.

Train for a Marathon
From Mr. Rothacker –

Changing the culture of an organization takes time...a lot of time. It also takes planning, patience, and determination with an eye towards the future. Although I am not a runner, my daughter was a Division I athlete in Track & Field. I would watch her train in the blazing heat, in the frigid cold, in the pounding rain, and even in the darkness of night. We would often pass each other on weekend mornings as I was going to the mailbox to retrieve the newspaper, and she was already returning from her morning workout at the gym. She would try to explain to me the euphoric feeling during a "runner's high." I have also seen her take several days off from her workout ritual after a poor race performance, as if she was giving up. However, I later learned that she was not giving up at all, but rather she was reflecting and analyzing what went wrong and revising her workouts and strategies to make the next race a winner. I learned so much from her.

I began to compare her experiences as a distance runner with my experiences as the leader of a school going through the trauma sensitive transformation process. We both needed to be planners, people who could look ahead to identify the obstacles and develop strategies to overcome them. We understood that there were going to be days when things could not get better and our goal appeared to be within an arm's reach, and other days where taking just one more step just seemed too exhausting. We both learned how much we can learn from setbacks and that the only time failure sets in is when you give up. As time went on, we saw our hard work begin to pay off which inspired us to work even harder than we thought possible.

A final note from Nathan Levy – Former principal, Director of Elementary Education, worldwide education consultant, and author of over sixty books.

It is important that trauma sensitive schools are not only trauma sensitive, but schools of excellence. Our "revolution" is not only to make us trauma sensitive – but more importantly, to make us excellent in helping all of our students learn and grow academically as thinkers, and literate contributors to society, their families, and communities. Every "lion" and "duck" is important to themselves and maybe to the world based upon the unlimited potential of our children.

There are many people in education who can spout what to do – but cannot do it. There will continue to be teachers and other school personnel who may not be able to "talk the talk" of trauma sensitivity – but may, in fact, be the most productive educators for our children. Some of the best players in baseball (basketball, football, etc.) could never explain how they hit a ball. We will continue to have many teachers with a natural propensity for reaching all kids – including those who have experienced trauma. The test for our success may not be on paper – but in the actual abilities to reach ducks and lions in ways that help them go forward into a bright future.

In Closing…..

The journey towards transforming your school is just that……It is a journey, and journeys take time. The difference with this journey is that there is no ending destination. You will always be working toward making your school more sensitive, more empathetic, more compassionate and more inclusive. However, there will come a time along the way when you feel a genuine sense of pride when you look around your school and witness the wonderful things your school has accomplished. You will see it and most importantly, you will feel it. That is your "runner's high" moment. It will come. Be patient, work hard, and continue to believe in your mission. We believe in you! Welcome to the revolution!

References

Alisic, E. (2012). Teachers' perspectives on providing support to children after trauma: A qualitative Study. School Psychology Quarterly, 27(1), 51-59. doi:10.1037/a0028590

Anda, R.F., Butchart, A., Felitti, V.J., & Brown, D.W. (2010). Current issue: Building a Framework for Global Surveillance of the Public Health *Implications of Adverse Childhood Experiences. American* Journal of Preventive Medicine, 3993-98. doi:10.1016/j.amepre.2010.03.015

Balfanz, R., Byrnes, V., & Fox, J. (2014) Sent home and put off-track: The antecedents, disproportionalities, and consequences of being suspended in the ninth grade. *Journal of Applied Research on Children: Informing Policy for Children at Risk, 5*(2),1-18. Retrieved from: http://digitalcommons.library.tmc.edu/childrenatrisk/vol5/iss2/13

Dorado, J., Martinez, M., McArthur, L., & Leibovitz, T. (2016). Health Environments and Response to Trauma in Schools (HEARTS): A school based, multi-level comprehensive prevention and intervention program for creating trauma-informed, safe, and supportive schools. School Mental Health. doi:10.1007/ s12310-016-9177-0.

Duke, N.N., Pettingell, S.L., McMorris, B.J., & Borowski, I.W. (2010). Associations with multiple types of adverse childhood experiences. *Pediatrics, 125*(4), 778- 786. doi:10.1542/peds.2009-0597

Fabelo, T., Thompson, M.D., Plotkin, M., Carmichael, D., Marchbanks, M.P.III, &   Booth, E.A. (2011). *Breaking schools' rules: A statewide study of how school discipline relates to students' success and juvenile justice involvement*. Council of State Governments Justice Center: New York. Retrieved from: http://csgjusticecenter.org/youth/breaking-schools-rules-report/

Finkelhor, D., Turner, H.A., Shattuck, A., & Hamby, S.L. (2013). Violence, crime, and abuse exposure in a national sample of children and youth: An update. *Journal of American Medical Association Pediatrics, 167*(7), 614-621. doi:10.1001/jamapediatrics.2013.42

Sadin, M. (2017). Perceptions of Special Education Teachers Regarding Trauma-Informed Care: A Qualitative Study (Doctoral Dissertation) ProQuest.

Sadin, M., Flox, C., & Levy, N. (2018).   *Resiliency Through the Arts.* Nathan Levy Publishing, LLC. Monroe Township, NJ.

Sadin, M., Laningham, A & Levy, N. (2018). *Gifted Children and How Trauma Affects Them.* Nathan Levy Publishing, LLC. Monroe Township, NJ.

Sadin, M & Levy, N. (2020). *Teachers' Guide to Trauma.* Nathan Levy Publishing, LLC. Monroe Township, N J.

Skiba, R. J. (2014). The Failure of Zero Tolerance. *Reclaiming Children & Youth, 22*(4), 27-33. Retrieved from: https://reclaimingjournal.com/node/1454

Melissa Sadin, Ed.D.

Executive Director: Ducks & Lions: Trauma Sensitive Resources
Program Director: Creating Trauma Sensitive Schools for The Attachment & Trauma Network
Special Ed. Director: Unity Charter School

Melissa has served as a special education teacher and a building administrator. She is currently working as a director of special education. Publicly, Dr. Sadin has been vice-president of her local School Board, is on the Board of Directors of the Attachment & Trauma Network and serves as the director of the Creating Trauma Sensitive Schools Program. She is a published author who produces numerous webinars on children with attachment trauma in schools. Currently, Dr. Sadin works as an education consultant and developmental trauma expert providing professional development to school districts, municipal service providers, and parents. As an adoptive mother, Dr. Sadin has provided first hand expertise in her work with adoptive parents at conferences and in other formal and informal settings.

Nathan Levy

Author & Consultant
President, Nathan Levy Books, LLC

Nathan Levy is the author of more than 60 books which have sold almost 500,000 copies to teachers and parents in the United States, Europe, Asia, South America, Australia and Africa. His unique <u>Stories with Holes</u> series continues to be proclaimed the most popular activity used in gifted, special education and regular classrooms by thousands of educators. An extremely popular, dynamic speaker on thinking, writing and differentiation, Nathan is in high demand as a workshop leader in school and business settings. He has worked as a school principal, district supervisor, gifted coordinator, is a company president, parent of four daughters and management trainer. Nathan's ability to transfer knowledge and strategies to audiences through humorous, thought provoking stories assures that participants leave with a plethora of new ways to approach their future endeavors. Nathan Levy Books, LLC is pleased to be the publisher of this book. More books available at www.storieswithholes.com

Ralph K. Rothacker

Director of Education – St. Anne's Institute, Albany, NY
Board of Directors, Vice President – Attachment & Trauma Network

Ralph has dedicated over thirty-five years to public education. His multiple degrees from the New York State University system has afforded him the unique opportunity to teach *and* serve as a school leader at the elementary, middle and high school levels. Ralph retired as a public-school administrator in 2013, and currently serves as the Director of Education at Saint Anne Institute, located in Albany, New York. St. Anne's is a residential and day service facility for adolescent girls who have been identified by the courts and public schools as "Difficult to Place". Ralph and his staff are committed to creating and maintaining a trauma sensitive school environment where all students feel safe and high academic expectations are achieved. As a keynote speaker, trainer and consultant Ralph works with schools across the nation to guide them through their journey towards creating trauma-based programming. Ralph is currently serving as the Vice-President of the Board of Directors for The Attachment and Trauma Network.

Dynamic Speakers
Creative Workshops
Relevant Topics

Nathan Levy, author of the *Stories with Holes* series, *Teachers' Guide to Trauma* and *Creativity Day By Day* and other nationally known authors and speakers, can help your school or organization achieve positive results with children. We can work with you to provide a complete in-service package or have one of our presenters lead one of several informative and entertaining workshops.

Workshop Topics Include:

- Differentiating in the Regular Classroom
- How to Help Children Read, Write and Think Better
- Powerful Strategies to Enhance the Learning of Gifted Students
- Powerful Strategies to Help Hard to Reach Students Become More Successful Learners
- Teachers' Guide to Trauma
- Arts and Resiliency
- Gifted and Trauma
- Brain Whys – How the Brain Works
- Adoption Competent Education
- IEP/504 Facilitation
                and many more…

Please write or call to receive our current catalog.
Nathan Levy Books, LLC
(732) 605-1643
NLevy103@comcast.net
www.storieswithholes.com

Unique Materials Published by
Nathan Levy Books, LLC

A.C.T. 1: Affective Cognitive Thinking
Artistry
Beyond Schoolwork
Brain Whys
Breakfast for the Brain
Creativity Day-By-Day
Gifted Children and How Trauma Impacts Them
Nathan Levy's Intriguing Questions – Volumes 1-6
Nathan Levy's Stories with Holes – Volumes 1-22
Nathan Levy's Test Booklet for Every American
Perfectionism vs. the Pursuit of Excellence
Principles of Fearless Leadership
School Leaders' Guide to Trauma Sensitive Schools
Teachers' Guide to Resiliency Through the Arts
Teachers' Guide to Trauma
The Principals Recommend: 101 Great Activities for
    Student Learning and Brain Development
There Are Those
Thinking & Writing Activities for the Brain- Bks 1 & 2
THINKology
Trauma Informed Teaching Strategies That Are Good For
    All
What To Do When Your Kid is Smarter Than You
Whose Clues? (Am. Hist., Mus., Lit., Sci., Sports, Authors)
Write from the Beginning

Ducks & Lions: Trauma Sensitive Resources
www.traumasensitive.com

Creating Trauma Sensitive schools for ALL children and the people who serve them.

- Creating Trauma Sensitive Schools - Professional Development
- Train-the-Trainer and Coaching models available
- IEP / 504 Facilitation for parents and schools
- Trauma-Informed Functional Behavior Assessment Services
- Gifted Activities that Work

Melissa Sadin – Executive Director
Melissa.sadin@gmail.com
@melissasadin

Melissa, Nathan and Ralph appreciate the Attachment & Trauma Network's support of families living with the impact of attachment disruption and childhood trauma.

ATN's Mission

At the Attachment & Trauma Network, it is our mission to:

Promote healing of traumatized children and their families through support, education and advocacy.

We Believe...

- We believe that traumatized <u>children</u> and those with attachment disorders <u>can heal</u>.
- We believe that <u>parents</u>, who are supported and taught therapeutic parenting, <u>are the best healing agents</u> of their traumatized child.
- We believe that traumatized children need <u>trauma-informed, attachment-focused therapies</u>.
- We believe that traumatized children learn best in <u>trauma-sensitive schools</u> where strategies are in place to help them feel safe, stay regulated and not be retraumatized or triggered.
- We believe that <u>providing resources</u> to the families <u>from the start</u> (once a traumatized child has been identified) is the best way to minimize crises and reduce disruptions and potential "rehoming".
- We believe that ongoing parent-to-parent <u>support is critical</u> in arming the families with strategies, tools and strength to persevere daily.
- We believe that "touching trauma at its heart" is more than a slogan...<u>it's a healing mission</u>.

We Believe in ATN.

CPSIA information can be obtained
at www.ICGtesting.com
Printed in the USA
BVHW030516141021
618748BV00012B/11

9 781410 102218